Girl from the Wrong Side of the Tracks

Alyce Weeden

Copyright © 2024 Alyce Weeden
All rights reserved.

ISBN 978-0-9999066-6-8

Written by: Alyce Weeden
Photography by: Alyce Weeden for Infinity Images
Edited by: Christina M. Berard, LMHC, LCDP, MAC
Project Managed by:
Jerrell Grimes Entertainment & Management Services LLC

Cover image under license. Used with permission.
Printed & distributed by: Amazon KDP

No part of this publication may be reproduced, distributed, or transmitted in any form or by any means, including photocopying, recording, or other electronic or mechanical methods, without the prior written permission of the author, except in the case of brief quotations embodied in critical reviews and certain other noncommercial uses permitted by copyright law. The names of people appearing in this work have been changed to protect privacy. Any similarity to actual people, living or dead, is purely coincidental.

Special discounts are available on quantity purchases by corporations, associations, and others (including U.S. trade bookstores, independent bookstores, and wholesalers). For permission requests, write to the publisher, or visit the publisher's website.

Ten19 Media Group LLC
Tampa, Florida
www.ten19mediagroup.com | info@ten19mediagroup.com

Printed in the United States of America

Girl from the Wrong Side of the Tracks

To my sons Jahmere & Amir,

I want you to finally know the true story of your mother and father. I want you to finally know our history and what occurred before you were born (and when you were younger).

I want you to know about our relationship during middle school and high school. I want you to know about the struggle thereafter…

Girl from the Wrong Side of the Tracks

Journal Entries

Innocence Stolen	7
Who Will Protect You?	15
Living Older Than My Age	21
School Days and Deception	27
Life Hits Hard	33
Life: Filled with Challenges	41
Weekend Visits and Work Life	53
Acting Grown	61
Setbacks and New Beginnings	69
Dealing Drugs Gets You Nowhere	77
Abuse and How It Changed Me	85
Placing Blame	93
Fake Friends & My Downfall	103
Self-Medicating	111

Innocence Stolen

It was fall, October to be exact, in Newport, Rhode Island. We were behind "The Rec." The leaves were turning, and the grass was wet. I recall another tragic event on Halloween night, after getting all my candy.

I ran into the bully who struck once again. Jacob found me walking by "The Rec.," which was a local basketball court and park. Behind the park was the Quaker Meeting House, a historic building. It was just me and Jacob. He told me to go with him. I hesitated because I knew what was going to happen to me. He threw my bookbag and pushed me to the wet ground. I smelled wet, moldy leaves while I was on the ground.

He yanked my stretch pants down to my ankles and pulled down his pants. He penetrated me without my consent. I said no, but he kept pumping until he finished. I felt wet and disgusted. I just wanted to rip out his braces. I recall having wet leaves all over my back and as I was pulling up my pants, he said, "You better not tell no one." I ran to my grandmother's house which was not too far from his house. When I got there, I showered and put my clothes in the laundry. I felt violated. I had a ton of candy, but I just went to bed and tried to cast out what just happened.

I woke up like usual. My cousin was talking to me about how much candy we had gotten while my nana made eggs, bacon, and pancakes. I was a good eater. In fact, I was on the chubby side and insecure about my body. Me and my cousin walked to school. I was in junior high, and he was in elementary school.

One might wonder why I was not staying with my mother, stepfather, sister, and brother. I did not feel loved or appreciated. I was always put on diets to control my weight. My mother always favored my sister because she was an honor student. My brother was out of control, and I did not feel it was up to me to take care of the family while they worked. So, I spent most of my time at my grandparents' house. The only downfall was Jacob lived right up the street which meant more sexual encounters.

One day at school, Jacob spread the word that I and two of my friends were "easy." Theresa was a big girl who had sex with a group of friends, and Gloria was a sex addict who loved performing sexual acts with these guys. She would brag about it. They both made a name for themselves, but I was reserved.

One day in Art class, Keith asked me if I could help him with his homework. He seemed nice enough. In hindsight, he was in that same group of friends. After school, we walked together and talked about school and classwork to pass the time. It was about a 20-minute walk to get to Freebody Park. When we got there, I tried to put my bag on the kitchen chair, but Keith said to follow him. We walked down a nice hallway decorated with family pictures. We came to a white door. He told me to watch my step;

Girl from the Wrong Side of the Tracks

I walked gingerly down the stairs. It smelled like a basement; moldy, damp and very unorganized. Keith led me to a section in the basement with low lighting and about three or four twin mattresses all spread out. They looked stained. The floor was wet. Keith said it was time to do our homework. He told me I was going to be his too. He threw me on the mattress. I tried to fight back but he was stronger than me. He got my jeans undone and began to penetrate me very roughly, but it would not fit. He forced it. It hurt so bad all I could do was cry and yell, "Stop!" He said, "Take it! You know you want it!" He heard his father come into the house and call his name.

"Keith? Keith, where are you? I see a book bag." Keith told me to hurry up, get up, and get dressed. I wiped my tears, terrified of getting caught in his house. He told me to wait on the steps and he would come back for me. It seemed like forever that I was waiting.

He finally came to me and told me to run! I grabbed my bag and ran two houses away and then walked fast. I jumped on a bus to get back to my mom's house. It seems like on that side of the tracks I am safe from sexual assault. I showered and had to deal with my sister who nagged about everything. My mom came home, and Dad ordered pizza. We all ate. There was no conversation about how my school day was. Instead, she asked my sister how Times Squared was (a math group for smart kids). Meanwhile, I had been raped twice and nobody knew.

The next morning, we were off to school. Breakfast was always cold cereal or, for my diet, rice cakes with peanut butter. The bus ride to school was quiet. There were a few kids on the bus. When I arrived at school, I started looking for Theresa and Gloria. I found them on the side of the courtyard. I found them with Erica which was strange because she usually spent time with the more popular students. I said hi to everyone. They greeted me back. Theresa and Gloria said they had to go. I knew that meant blow jobs before school in the boy's gym. I did not go. The last thing I wanted was to be in that type of situation. Erica and I chopped it up and then she invited me to her house after school. I said, "OK" and got the address.

The school day went off without a hitch for me, but the boys were talking about how Theresa is a beast and how good her blow job was. They called Gloria the beast because she swallowed and took it up the ass. I was listening to what they were saying, and I was disgusted. I would never want a group of students talking about me like that. That faded away and we got on with our school day. The last bell rang. I caught up to Erica and we walked to her house. It was only 5 minutes away. We walked into a nice, neat, beautifully decorated apartment.

Erica got me something to drink and went upstairs to bring her things. I heard someone running down the stairs. It was Jayceon, her brother. He was very handsome and caught my eye. He greeted me with, "What's up?" I said, "Nothing much, just waiting on Erica." He asked me if I could come back later. I was like, "Uh huh, yes, sure. Why do you want me to come back?" Jayceon said, "I just want to talk to you without my sister here." I agreed. He was so sexy. He was tall, milk chocolate, had a beautiful smile, and manners. Wow! I could not wait until Erica had to go to work. She came back downstairs in her work clothes. We sat and watched *Yo! MTV Raps*, we commented on a few rap artists and then I left.

Theresa lived on the main strip of West Broadway, so I just walked over there. I knocked on the door, she answered. I asked her what she was doing in a little while. She said she wasn't doing anything and asked why. I asked if I could leave my bag there for a little while because I had to go somewhere. Theresa asked where I was going. I told her I would tell her later. She told me not to do anything she would not do. I never replied and walked down the stairs.

I walked out the door, went around the corner, and rang the doorbell. Jayceon opened the door with a smile and said, "Come in." He asked me if I would like anything to eat or drink. I asked for juice. He handed me my juice and asked if I would like to go upstairs and listen to music. I agreed and asked if he was going to hurt me. He said, "Alexis, no I am not like that." I replied, "Okay, my trust is low these days." We sat on the bed and drank juice, as we listened to Sade, some old school artist. It was smooth. The lights were dim. I was thinking it was going to happen. I wanted to have sex with him for some reason.

He was a true gentleman in the way he came on to me. He held my hands, softly kissed my lips and I kissed him back. He proceeded to lift my jean skirt and slide my underwear down slowly. He lifted my legs all the way onto the bed. He then asked if I was okay. I replied, "Yes." We began to have sex and for the first time, I thought in my head this was how it should be. Both parties agreed; it was very pleasurable.

I thanked him for being gentle. Jayceon replied, "I'm not like most dudes you will meet." We parted ways with a kiss. I left and went back to Theresa's house, knocked on the door. She and Gloria were sitting in the living room. I walked in and joined them. They did not ask me much, but I was not offering any information either. I did not want them to steal my new boo thing. Nothing much was talked about other than them going to John's house tomorrow after school to drink. They asked me if I wanted to go. I said, "Yeah, why not?" I headed back to my grandmother's house for the night. When I got there, I ate, took a shower, and went to bed.

My alarm went off the next day. I grabbed something that was already pressed. I got dressed, brushed my teeth, washed my face, and went downstairs ready to eat breakfast. My nana made French toast, eggs, sausage, and strawberry milk.

Girl from the Wrong Side of the Tracks

Off to school I went. I told both of my grandparents I loved them and to have a good day. As usual, I had time to chat with the girls about going to John's this afternoon. I was trying to find out who was going to be there. All they would say was "a bunch of us." I told them I would meet them there; I had to go home first and put away my school stuff. During school, Jacob approached me and asked me if I was going to John's party. I told him I wasn't sure yet because I had things to do. He was the last person I ever wanted to talk to. He would find a way to hang out with my cousin, and I would be forced to have sex with him. I liked him up until he raped me that Halloween night. At this point, he made my stomach turn.

I was walking home to my grandmother's house. He saw me, grabbed me up, and forced me into his house. I yelled to leave me alone, but no one heard my cry for help. He made me go to the basement where he was watching pornography and because I would not copy what they were doing, he put me in the closet. It was dark. I was scared. I did not know if he was going to rape me again. I pleaded with him to let me out. He did, but then he punched me in the back of my head and threw me on the couch and said, "I know you had sex with Jayceon and Keith!! You don't think we talk? Now I am showing you that you are just mine." He took off my pants and did his business. I just laid there crying. I got up and got dressed and walked to my grandmother's house, wiping my tears away. She was in the back room where she watched the kids. I said hello to all the kids and my grandmother. I just went to the bathroom to wash up with Coast soap and hot water. I dried myself off and put on clean underwear.

Girl from the Wrong Side of the Tracks

Who Will Protect You?

I was on the search for my father, who, by 4:00, was done with work and could be in one or two places: at home or on the hunt for crack cocaine and alcohol. I saw him on Broadway, the main street that runs through Newport. He was coming from the liquor store. I yelled, "Dad!!!!" He turned around when he heard me and started to walk towards me. As I walked up to him, I told him I had to tell him something important. We walked down the street and sat down in front of the police station. With a look of astonishment, he did not know what to expect. I told him Jacob Smith has forced me to have sex with him on several occasions.

My dad agreed to walk to Tilden Avenue, a small, tight side street in Newport where Jacob lived. It took us about ten minutes because we were walking fast. When we got there, I rang the bell and Jacob answered. I told him I told my dad about him and how he forced me to have sex with him. He said, "Man you know I would never do that to your daughter. We just played around, and she's mad because I accidently hit her in the head today." My dad looked at me and said, "You better stop lying because he is a family friend and would not do that to you." Then, my dad had the audacity to ask him if he had anything, meaning my dad really brought me on a crack deal and did not believe me. Jacob asked him how much he was looking for. My dad wanted a $50 piece.

They exchanged money for crack cocaine. He told Jacob, "Good looking out man. I will talk to her."

I said, "Dad he is lying! Why don't you believe me?" He said, "It is just a teenage misunderstanding. Go to your grandmother's and eat dinner." We parted ways. I walked around the corner to Appleby Street, which was where my grandmother lived, a small side street with two-way traffic. All I could think about as I walked was that my dad didn't believe me. He was a crackhead alcoholic who didn't believe his own daughter. If the man I put on a pedestal didn't believe me, then no one would believe me.

I missed John's party because of all this so I will have to find out what happened tomorrow at school. I walked into the house; it smelled so good. I asked my nana what she was making. She replied to me, "Pork chops and gravy, with onions, over white rice, and corn bread muffins." I sat at the table until she told me to go wash my hands. My cousin walked in and washed his hands. We sat and got ready to be served. He whispered to me, "Do you want mine?" I said, "Yeah." He picked around his plate at the green beans. I worked on my entire plate. I devoured it. We swapped plates. I was on round two and thought to myself I was self-medicating with food. I ate at a slower pace. I finished it all up and washed it down with sweet tea.

I stayed in that night. It was my dish night. We had to hand wash, rinse the dishes, and dry them with a kitchen cotton towel. Man,

Girl from the Wrong Side of the Tracks

I hated when it was my dish night, but I ate good. I took a shower around 7:00 pm after I did the dishes. I just kept thinking that I was going to get raped and beaten every day. I never knew my cousin portrayed the friendship as just Jacob and I hanging out. I pressed my clothes for the next day. After that, I set my alarm and went to bed.

I woke up the next morning, brushed my teeth, washed my face, and went back to my room to put on my clothes. I went to the breakfast table and was disappointed. It was left over corn bread muffins, and they were rock hard after sitting out all night. They were served with beans and bacon, one of my grandfather's go to breakfasts when he was able to cook. I ate and left for school.

I walked down Tilden. Jacob must have left early because he was nowhere in sight walking to school. I went to Cotay's Pharmacy where all the school kids went on Broadway to get "5 and dime" candy, potato chips, and soda. I saw Big Mark, tall and dark with big lips. We picked out our candy and he made small talk about Hip Hop music. He told me to pick out whatever I wanted because he was paying. I got a couple of Now and Laters and some Doritos. We checked out and walked to school.

Thomson Jr. High School was a building that needed to be updated. It had leaks and smelled awful. I cannot even describe the smell other than smelling old and moldy. Mark and I talked in the courtyard. I could tell he liked me; he asked me if I had a boyfriend. I said, "No. Why?" He said, "Because I want you to be my girlfriend." I said, "Let me think about it." As we walked off together, he grabbed my hand. I felt comfort, like I was a little lady that had this 6-foot boy protecting me.

The school day went on without a problem. In my last class, I asked to use the bathroom. I ran into Mark in the hallway. He said, "Alexis, did you think about what I asked you?" I told him I did. He said, "Well?" I said, "Yes, I will be your girlfriend." He had to bend to hug me because I am only 5-feet, 7 inches. Mark told me to go to his house after school to watch him DJ. I asked where he lived. He told me the address. It was right around the corner from Theresa, off West Broadway, in the new houses. This is the same area where I hung out with Jayceon. It's a small community of mixed incomes and got the name the "New Houses," which meant it was a big circle of chaos. Theresa, Jayceon, and Mark were all within walking distance and they were all friends with Jacob and Keith.

I remember watching him DJ. It was Shabba Ranks, a Reggae album. He would cut and scratch on the turn tables. We were in his room. He said, "I have to go across the street to my aunt's house. No one is home, you will be okay. I'll play the record for you."

It seemed like five minutes and then I heard someone run up the stairs. I looked at the door, it's Jacob! I screamed, "Get out! Mark

Girl from the Wrong Side of the Tracks

is not here!" He said, "I told you, you're mine!" He took off my pants, humped me until he relieved himself, and then left. When Mark came back, I told him what happened. He ran outside and started fighting Jacob on Kingston Ave. Fists were flying, they were tussling to the ground. It was so scary, but I had a sense of happiness that Jacob was getting what he deserved. When the fight was over, Mark said, "Do not ever violate my girl, Alexis, like that you punk ass motherfucker!" Mark took me back in the house and said, "What happened was not nice. I fought for you. I'll protect you from anyone who ever tries to hurt you." This was exactly what I needed. I needed someone to put an end to my abuse. I started to wonder if my friends were also being abused by the same boys. No teenager should have to go through all the abuse I went through. No teenager should be neglected or ignored by their parent who chose to ignore my pain because of drugs. I blame my dad for not sticking up for me, for not protecting me.

Living Older Than My Age

The relationship I had with Mark is one I won't forget. We spent the summer together. I worked at Burger King on Thames Street, a main cobblestone road in downtown Newport. It was surrounded by shops such as the Music Box (which sold records, tapes, and CDs) and The Army Navy Surplus (which sold clothes, military clothing, and other products). It was always busy in the summer with car and foot traffic going to all these shops. I rode my bike to work every day and anywhere I went. Most of my time was spent at work or with Mark and several of my other older friends. I babysat for my friend Tanya on different nights and partied with her and some of my older friends on other nights.

Let's go back to Mark. He was a drug dealer. He always had a pocket full of money and dressed to the nines (meaning the latest footwear, brand name clothing, car and moped). Mark had it all. His mother was absent due to going to nursing school. His brother ran around the neighborhood and told me everything. His stepfather did drugs and was alcoholic. One thing I knew was I was accepted there. I was a girl from the wrong side of the tracks.

The summer was hot and muggy. He lived in a three-bedroom townhouse with no air conditioning. He had a fan in his room.

We were like sex machines. Mark fed my desire for sex. There was nothing that we did not explore sexually. Oral sex, anal sex. It was just a passionate, sexual relationship. I knew he loved me, and I loved him. He always made sure I was protected from those assholes who raped me.

I always had thousands of dollars in my pocket: I began to buy better clothes, make-up, and the latest shoes such as, Nike, K-Swiss, and Timberlands for the winter. We spent the summer drinking. He smoked weed; I didn't do that drug. One Friday night after work, I went to my grandmother's, showered and parked my bike. My aunt Lea asked me if I wanted to go drink at my friend Tanya's house. She told my nana I was babysitting, and I would be home tomorrow morning.

We went to my friend's house. The music was on blast, there were cases of 40 oz (about 1.18L) malt beer in the fridge. They had a funnel for a game. I grabbed my St. Ides (malt beer) and began to drink. At first, I thought it was nasty, but the feeling it gave me, I loved. There was a house full of niggas (meaning older black men of color). They all knew I was Lea's niece. It was my turn to make a boiler maker (which was malt beer and vodka).

I put the funnel to my mouth and a friend poured my beer in the funnel until I raised my hand to stop. It was a lot of beer, but I could swallow it like I was a pro. Then it was time for the boiler maker, a shot glass of vodka and a beer in a regular glass, I drank it down without hesitation. I was feeling tipsy.

An older male friend asked me to go outside. The porch was kind of dark with only dim porch lights on in the neighborhood. He tongue-kissed me forcefully and rubbed my body down. I broke away from him and went back into the house to drink my beer.

Mark was next door at a girl's house. They said we looked similar. She had a different walk and a gap between her legs. She had a brother that was gay and around his brother's age. Little did I know he would come to Mark's house. They would have sex, along with a few of his neighborhood friends.

As I mentioned, Mark had a car. He would go on "runs" and leave me for hours. I found out later there was an older woman in the picture who was crack head. Yeah, they fucked. Newport is small and word spreads. That summer, I confronted him about cheating. He denied it. I felt some type of way and kept to myself.

I went out with Aunt Lea to the Pineapple Pub with her ID because we looked a tad bit similar. We were the same height, but she was a little chubbier than me. Another lie told to my nana. I was dressed in a short, black miniskirt with a top with see-through arms. It had roses on the front and back. I wore black wedges and make-up.

My Aunt Lea was more of a tomboy. She wore jean shorts and an orange cotton top with Adidas. We drank in her room and then we walked to the club around 10. My nana was always upstairs by nine after checking downstairs. My aunt would unlock the back door so I could get in after the club in case my nana came downstairs. It took about ten minutes to get to the alley where the club was. The alley was close to West Broadway. It stunk like piss, had broken bottles, trash on the ground and a dumpster. The cool thing was black people and other nationalities hung out there. This was the time when the Navy had a heavy presence in Newport. They say Newport girls loved Navy men.

We walked down the staircase to get in. I was carded but I made it in. I don't remember the music, but it had to be early to late 80's music. People standing were standing everywhere, some were sitting at the crowded bar. I stuck close to Aunt Lea. We made it to the bar. She ordered vodka and cranberry juice, and I ordered the same. We paid for our drinks and started to mingle and talk. She introduced me to one of her navy friends. We began to talk and danced where we were standing. He bought me another drink.

The conversation was going well for a 15-year-old and a grown sailor. Out of nowhere, Mark snatched me up and asked, "What the fuck are you doing here?" I said, "Just chilling.' He says, "Oh no you are not, let's go!" We got to the door, and he told the door man not to let me in because I was underage.

Girl from the Wrong Side of the Tracks

We rode back to his house on a moped. It was a tight squeeze. We got off the moped, walked into his house and went upstairs. He ripped off my skirt angrily, busted open my shirt, pushed me to the bed, and had sex with me. This was the first time I thought he was like the other boys who raped me. He said my aunt was a whore and asked me if I was trying to be a whore just like her. I said, "No. I'm not a whore! I am me! I just wanted to go to the club." He said, "Yeah and fuck that navy dude you were talking to. I peeped the whole scene." There was not much more I could say. I never knew he went to the Pineapple Pub.

I slept over. The next morning, I walked all the way to grandmother's house super early. When I walked in, she asked me what I was doing. I lied and told her I went to the store. She didn't give me any flack.

School Days and Deception

Fast forward to the first day of 7th grade. Mark was on the football team. He was popular even though he transferred in 6th grade from North Kingstown Jr. High School. I was in classes for students who did not try. The kids were mouthy and disrespectful, including me. I never took home a book. I did most of my homework in class. I went to Mark's games when I did not have to work at Burger King.

I went back to staying with my mother and stepfather who I also call "Dad." He and my mom have been together since I was in 2nd grade. They got married when I was in 5th grade. No one knew I had a drug dealing boyfriend or a pocket full of cash. I was just a girl from the wrong side of the tracks. One of my cousins moved in. We were the same age and in the same grade. She was tall, slender, pretty, and had long curly hair. My mom's sister had some type of arrangement for her to come live with us.

My mom knew she dated a black boy for a short time. He was a drug dealer wannabe. Then she was with the white boy who piqued her interest. He lived in the white house outside the building complex we lived in, on the second floor.

We all shared a room together. I had my own dresser and a 50lb laundry bag I lived out of when I lived with my mom. It was always messy on my side. My biological sister had a bottom bunk and white Persian cat that lived on her bed. I had a twin bed on the left side. My cat was black and orange with long hair. My cousin took the closet for her clothes and had the top bunk. We shared the bottom of the closet for shoes.

We started school in September, after Labor Day. It was still warm out, the last taste of summer. There were cool mornings, warm afternoons, and chilly nights. I rode the bus with my cousin's crush. I knew everybody. When we got to school, all the girls met in a hallway to chat about things that were going on. Then, I would walk with my cousin to the second floor before we split to go to our homerooms.

One day, Mark greeted me at the door of my homeroom with a kiss before running off to his homeroom. He told me he would see me after school. That day, someone gave me a note from Theresa saying I should go to Mark's game the next day. When I asked her why, she said, "You'll see."

It was homecoming time. Mark didn't ask me to go. I had just assumed he was too grown to be going to a school dance. Instead of getting on the bus, I told my cousin I was staying for make-up work because I was good for that.

Mark and I walked to his house. I met his older sister who did not live with them. She was in a group home for girls in Portsmouth, Rhode Island, which was about a 25-minute drive from his house. We chatted and instantly clicked. She was funny.

Girl from the Wrong Side of the Tracks

I could tell that they loved each other by the way they horse played and giggled. It was never said why she was in a group home for girls. She left, but on her way out she said, "Bye, sis." I said, "Bye, nice to meet you."

His brother was there in the kitchen and of course, he just had something to tell me. He said, "My brother is going to homecoming, but you didn't hear it from me." I was flustered but managed to ask who he was going with. His reply was, "Just wait! You will see." I was pissed off.

I said, "Mark let's go upstairs, I want to talk." We made our way up the stairs and into the room. He locked the door, and we laid on the unmade bed. When I asked him if he was going to homecoming, he lied and said, "No, why?" I said, "I'm just asking because you know I have to work. You have not even bothered to ask me." Mark said, "That's because I know you work on Friday nights." I said, "Well, if you would have asked me weeks ago then I could have taken it off. Two different people are telling me that you're going without me." I knew he was lying to me, so I dropped the subject and planned in my head to investigate the bullshit.

When I went to his game the next day, he wasn't expecting me. I saw him talking to another girl down in the stands before practice. She was light skinned, thin, kind of pretty, with a MC Lyte haircut (a female rapper from the late 80's). I went down to the bottom of the stands and the expression on both of their faces was priceless- a deer caught in headlights.

She said, "Hi, Alexis." I said, "Hi, what's going on?" She said, "Nothing, we were just talking about my brother, Keith." The near mention of Keith's name disrupted my whole train of thought.

I found Theresa and asked if my surprise was to catch him with her. She said, "Girl! That isn't even half of it. I heard they were messing around." I was so pissed I walked to Broadway, bought some Chinese rice and ribs, caught the bus home, and didn't even bother to talk to Mark for the rest of the day.

Needless to say, I had an attitude when I finally got home. Mom and dad were at work. It was just me and my cousin in the bedroom. I told her who I was dating. She said, "Wow, him?" I said, "Yes. Is he bad news? Do you know stuff about him?" She asked, "Do you know about Lauren that rides our bus?" I said, "No. What is he doing with her?" She said, "Dating her and you are too." I never had a reason to think he was cheating so this was shocking. All I could do was cry. She hugged me and said she would show me the next day.

The next morning at the girls' gathering, Mark and I were the topic of conversation. I was so upset! When my cousin pointed her out, I said, "She is an ugly ass bitch! I should beat her ass." They all held me back. After we departed the bus, I confronted her and asked if she was messing with Mark. She was startled and said, "No, we are just good friends." I said, "If I find out any different, you've got an ass whooping coming." My cousin and I walked around the school to the store to grab some candy, chips and a drink. I paid for it all.

When we left the store, Mark was bopping down the street. I told her to go, and I waited for him. When he approached me, I told him we had to break up. He asked, "What for? Hell no!" I said, "Between yesterday and today, I'm done." As I walked off, I could hear him yelling my name. I got far away from him and entered school. I had a bad day at school. I was mouthy to one of my teachers. I got kicked out of math class which was the last period of the day. Mark tried to call my house phone several times, but I had enough. I was done.

Girl from the Wrong Side of the Tracks

Life Hits Hard

It was Friday night, homecoming night, and I was at work. I worked my shift and rode my bike to Mark's house. His brother was there and ready to tell me all I wanted to hear. He told me about Mark going to homecoming with that girl from practice. He showed me the instant camera photo. Mark wore a white suit and red bow tie, and she wore a black and white polka dotted dress.

I was hurt to say the least. He told me where they went to dinner, but I don't recall the name of the place. There was a picture of him, her, and his mom standing in front of a brown lattice at a restaurant. I asked his brother about Lauren. He said there was an ugly, bucktooth, dark haired girl in a purple car that goes over when I wasn't there. I told him we broke up and didn't care what Mark did anymore.

When I left, I rode my bike through the buildings. Guess who I saw? Jayceon. I rode up to him and said hello. He said, "Hello stranger, what are you up to?" I said, "Nothing much, just trying to sort out some bullshit." He asked me if I wanted to come in for a little while. I said, "Sure, why not? I do not have anything to do." I brought my bike to his dining room. Jayceon asked me if I wanted to go upstairs. I remembered the last time, so I said yes. He turned the lights off and said, "I know you might say no because of Mark, but I want your body." I said, "I want you too."

I sat on his bed. I felt him close to me. He leaned in with the most passionate kiss.

He took my clothes off. As I undressed him, I kissed his chest and neck. We began to have sex. It wasn't just sex, in my mind, it was payback to Mark. We gave each other oral sex. It was so satisfying to my soul, I had chills.

When we were finished, I went to the bathroom to clean up. Then we went downstairs, had some small talk and he gave a kiss goodbye. He opened the back door and I got on my bike and rode home. I always had the curfew of 9'oclock. It was just a short ride, and I was fast on my bike. I made it home like nothing had happened.

I said hello to everyone outside, brought my bike up to the second floor, and opened the door with my key. Everyone was home in their rooms. I showered and went to bed. I had some thoughts of what I did. Part of me thought I was wrong, then there was another part that felt justified for all that Mark put me through.

It got harder for me to stay in school. I started to leave the school and go Easton's Beach which is a far walk from Thomspon Jr. High School (now Thompson Middle School).

I would sit at the beach and watch the waves crash against the rocks. There I had thoughts of suicide.

Girl from the Wrong Side of the Tracks

It was very hard in those moments. I thought about being raped, drinking, and my relationship issues with Mark. I knew in my heart that all these stories were true but facing them head on was another story. I left school so much they called my mother.

Finally, I confided in my mother and told her I went to the beach to clear my thoughts. She was finally present, meaning listening to me. I told her I felt like committing suicide. She called a crisis line that day in school. I talked to a woman who sounded very kind and understanding. I would not open to her about the root of the problems. I just said I was depressed and left it at that.

A therapist and counselor were assigned to me. I couldn't open up to the therapist because I was scared to talk again; that she wouldn't believe me. The counselor took me fishing. It was nice to have someone to generally talk to about life as a teenager. I kept my issues locked inside of me. I saw her for the remainder of the school year.

I stopped leaving school. Mark kept doing whatever he wanted. We got back into a relationship that was unhealthy but kept me sexually satisfied. I gave up on fighting girls and confronting them. I was in the relationship because he protected me. I would be financially well off. I didn't know it was causing more harm than good.

We went through the whole 8th grade like that until his mom threw him out because her house got raided for drugs. I'll never forget it. It was a crisp, fall day in 1991. Luckily, he didn't get arrested. He came to my house, which he never did because my mom didn't know he was my boyfriend. She thought I was dating Jacob Smith because he would always call my house. Mark came into the house. We sat down in the dining room, and he told me his mom kicked him out and he needed a place to stay.

I called my mom into the dining room and introduced them. It went well. Mark was very pleasant, and my mom welcomed him. I told her we were in school together and how his mother threw him out. My mom was in shock! She couldn't believe a mother would throw her son out on the streets.

I asked my mom if we could at least put him up for a week so he could go to school and give him and his mom some time to resolve their differences. My mom agreed and discussed the rules: we had the same curfew; he had to sleep on the couch; he couldn't be in my room unless the door was open. She said he could stay for one week. We both agreed to the stipulations.

My mom left the room, and we called a cab to pick us up so he could get some clothing. The cab came and it's a guy we called "One Light." He smoked cigarette after cigarette. The cab was so smokey and smelly. The ride was about five minutes. Mark paid the fare, and we got out of the cab. Mark still had the keys to his house and his mom was not home. I saw the aftermath of the drug raid and began to put the living room and kitchen back together.

Mark went upstairs to get some clothes and whatever else he needed. The house was in total disarray. I began to fix the furniture and hang up some of the curtains that were torn down. I fixed all the décor on the tables. I went into the dining room and fixed the chairs around the table and placed placemats. The kitchen was the worst. Everything was pulled out of the cabinets; broken glass was everywhere. It was very tricky to put things back to where they belonged because I only cooked there once.

I put all the pots and pans away. Then, I worked my way to the upper cabinets with bowls, glasses, and cups. There were boxes of open food tossed on the floor, some spilled out. I put the food back in the cabinet neatly. I swept the floor and mopped it. The house downstairs was put together like nothing had happened. Then, I saw the half bathroom with things outside the medicine cabinet and the cabinet below. I put that all together. "Whew! That was a lot," I thought to myself. I wondered if selling drugs was worth it.

I went upstairs. Mark was putting together his room which was also a disaster. Shelves tipped over, clothes everywhere. So, I joined in and helped him. He did the full bath and his brother's room. The only room left was his mom's room, and that was not too bad. I made his mom's bed while he picked up things the police had tossed around. It took us about two hours to put everything in order, hoping his mom would appreciate it and think about him going home.

When Mark finished packing his things, we called a cab back to my house. They said the cab would be there in 20 minutes, so Mark had the idea to have a quick sexual encounter. Soon after, the cab arrived and dropped us back at my house.

Mark paid the fare, and we ran into my building because of the rain. When we got into my house, Mark put his stuff in the front closet. We hung out all day because it was Saturday, and my parents were at work. All of us kids were in the house. I ordered 3 pizzas – pepperoni, sausage, and green peppers, and a bottle of Pepsi.

My brother was in his room playing video games and my sister and cousin were in the room cleaning up their area of the room. The pizza took thirty-five minutes to come. When it arrived, I called everyone to the dining room. We all grabbed paper plates and a glass and sat around the table and talked. Only my cousin knew he was a drug dealer at the time.

Mark stayed with my family for four days. He went to school and adhered to the rules and most importantly, no drug dealing. There was also no sex for four days. He was only allowed in my room while my parents were home and with the door open. He worked things out with his mom. Turns out, it was not just the raid. It was money and foodstamps.

Life: Filled with Challenges

After school, we parted ways and Mark went home with his belongings. I saw him in school the next day. I misread my schedule and showed up to work for no reason. I left and rode my bike to Mark's house. When I got there, a purple car was parked outside. I put my bike on the porch and went inside. He was inside eating Chinese food with some white girl! I asked, "Who the hell are you?"

He said, "This is my friend from Rogers High School." I said, "No, what is your name?" She said her name was Kathy. "Why are you sitting here with my man eating? Don't you know I am his girlfriend!!" Kathy said she didn't know about me. Now Mark was in the hot seat. I could see him getting uncomfortable about the situation and being caught between two women.

Mark had enough and told us both to leave. When it was just us on the porch, I confronted her. I knew it wasn't the first time she'd been there. She kept saying she was just his friend and didn't see why it was a problem. Finally, I told her she could have him and warned her that she's not the only one.
She stormed off.
To be honest, I wanted to smack the shit out of her. I walked into his house and went off on him. I told him he was nothing but a user, a liar, and a cheater. I told him I was done going

through this. He had the nerve to say that I was his number one and the rest of the girls don't really matter to him. I said, "Mark, if they do not matter, then why bother with them?" Mark replied, "I do not know why." I said, "Here we go again. We are breaking up until you can figure this shit out! I can be alone; I do not need you!" Then, I walked out, took my bike off the porch, and rode home.

On my ride I was thinking and feeling depressed once more; the feeling never truly goes away but situations like this just made it harder on me. I made it home. As soon as I walked through the door, my cousin told me my mom wanted to talk to me when she got home from work. I asked, "About what?" She replied with, "I am not sure. I just know she is mad." I told her I wasn't worried about what she had to say because I did not do anything wrong.

My mom got home from work about five o'clock and I could see the look on her face. She told me to go into the living room and sit down. I went in and sat down on the orange chair with a heavy wood frame. We had a parrot. He kept repeating my brother's name. My mom came in and sat down. She asked me if there was anything I wanted to tell her. I told her I didn't have anything on my mind.

Very sternly she asked me why I didn't tell her Mark was a drug dealer. I asked her who told her that and she replied with, "Do not worry about it. I am telling you right now that you are not allowed to be friends with him. And to be honest, I do not believe you that he is just your friend. He is your boyfriend and you have been keeping it from me."

I said, "Yes, mom, he is my boyfriend and we have been dating for a while now!" My mom said, "Oh great! That is just what you need - a drug dealing, low life for a boyfriend! That is it, I am calling the OBGYN to put you on birth control. All I need is for you to get pregnant. You have been missing your appointments with your counselor and therapist. Why is that?" I said, "Because it is dumb and pointless. Just leave me alone."

She said, "Watch your tone! I am not going to deal with you and your bullshit. I will tell you this! You better stop leaving school. You are to clean that mess of a room you have." Then I said, "You are always picking on me! You do not even love me. I am like a useless piece of crap to you!" Her reply was, "Well, if you weren't so difficult, we wouldn't be having this conversation!"

I told her I wanted to live with my grandmother. She said, "If you go anywhere, it will be your cousin's house where you can get yourself together. Don and Anette will take you and you will live with them. You can go to your grandmother's house on the weekends. I give up on you. You do not listen, and you are dating a drug dealer. I have zero tolerance for you!"

I screamed, "Fine, call them! I'll pack my stuff! I know where I am not wanted." She called them and arranged for me and my stuff to be picked up. I could not believe my own mom was giving up on me and sending me to live with my cousin, his wife, and kids. I went to my room and packed all my stuff. I had several trash bags and a laundry bag. I waited in my room until they came. I cried my eyes out.

I was just existing in a damaged shell of a body. My own mom did not even show me love. I thought maybe it was tough love but whatever it was, it was wrong. It took my cousin about forty-five minutes to arrive. We packed the car, and I rode my bike with my school backpack. It had my work clothes inside. I rode for about twenty minutes or so to Chapel Terrace which was a low-income housing project near the beach.

Some of my friends lived there so I was not new to the area. I got to my cousin's house, and I walked into the kitchen from the front door. The kitchen was dirty. There were dishes in the sink and all my stuff piled up near a wood kitchen table with mismatched chairs. The living room was very tidy with old furniture.

You could clearly tell from both the kitchen and the living room that they did not care about anything fancy. I would now be living with four other girls, me being the oldest and them ranging in age, from 2 years old to 10 years old. I called Annette "aunty" even though she was my cousin's wife. I asked her where I was going to put my stuff. She said in the room up the stairs on the right-hand side. There were three beds in that room. She told me to take the bed near the wall.

I began to unpack my things; my little cousins were watching me, asking me tons of questions while playing with their toys. Once unpacked, I sat on the firm bed with one pillow. I was still in shock from my mother throwing me out. I began to wonder what was going to happen to me here. I got called downstairs, so I walked down the wood staircase and sat in the living room. My aunt Annette and cousin Don said we were going to go over the rules of the house.

My cousin Don said, "You must go to school every day and stay the entire day. Secondly, you have the same curfew as your mom imposed of nine o'clock, no exceptions. You will do your own laundry and be here for dinner except for when you are working. You will alternate weekends with your grandmother's house and your mom's house. We are here to get you back on track with your therapy and bridge the gap between you and your mother and father." I said, "Okay that all seems reasonable."

My aunt Annette said, "Every other night is your dish night, and you must make sure the kitchen is cleaned. You may use the phone until nine thirty at night." I then said, "Okay, I can do that; I just have one question. Do you know that I am dating Mark?"

They both said, "Yes, we just ask that you be open and honest with us. I told them we were on the outs but that could change any time.

Our sit down was complete. I used the telephone to call Mark to tell him I had moved in with my cousin in Chapel Terrace and must alternate weekends with my mom. He said he would see me in school and that he hoped it would all work out for me. I hung up the phone and sat and watched tv with the girls until bedtime. I woke up at six for a shower. It was nice, hot, and steamy. I used a small sliver of soap to wash up. I could not recognize the smell of the soap. It smelled like cocoa butter mixed with something. I got dressed in my shorts and a red T-shirt with my red Nikes. I headed downstairs where my aunt Annette was waiting. She asked me if I wanted my hair braided.

I was amazed and said yes and asked for a French braid. We talked while she did a quick French braid. She told me how she loved to do hair and anytime I wanted my hair done to just ask. I thanked her and told her it was beautiful. My own mother was a hairdresser, and she would not braid my hair. I phoned Donna to tell her I was ready for school and that she could come over when she was ready. She would get me when she was done with her hair. We both lived in Chapel Terrace in the Southeast end of Newport, near Memorial Boulevard, a main street to all the beaches and shops. Bellevue Ave, an intersecting street, is where the mansions are.

Girl from the Wrong Side of the Tracks

You would not expect a low-income project complex to be located there. They were all brick buildings with four apartments in a block, all with hunter green doors that were glass with paint in the window. Donna arrived and we took the 10-minute walk to school. We lived too close for a school bus. Thank God we were headed into summer months and the weather was nice enough to wear shorts. We had one thing in common, our boyfriends were drug dealers.

We arrived at school and walked to our classes. I saw Mark and he apologized about cheating on me and asked if we could please work it out. I told him that we would have to talk about it after school. He asked me, "Can you please come over today?" I agreed to walk home with him.

The school day passed, and I made it through the day without leaving or getting in trouble. Mark and I walked to this house after school. We got into the apartment and went straight upstairs to his room. He turned on the music and then he started the conversation with, "I know I have played you (meaning cheated on you). I did not mean it. Those other girls do not mean anything to me. I know it seems like I am not considering how you feel. I just want to know you are my number one, and I love you."

As I sat on his bed and listened intently, I felt as if he meant every word of his apology. Also, in the back of my mind I felt as if this was not the end, and he was going to keep cheating. I was very vulnerable at this point because we had been through so much and I was leading with my heart and sexual desires. Before speaking, I thought about what I was going to say. I said to Mark, "I accept your apology because I love you and want to be with you. I want us to be exclusive; no cheating, no more lies."

He said, "Alexis, I can give you that. I've changed. I just want you to believe in me." I said, "I do believe in you. You got to be willing to have a solid relationship. We can try. Just be straight forward with me." He agreed. It was nearing dinner time. I told him I had to go and asked him if he wanted to walk me home. Mark said, "yes, anything for you." He gave me a wad of money. I did not even count it. I just put it in my pocket and thanked him.

On our way to my aunt's house, we talked about him selling drugs. I asked him when (and if) he was going to stop. He said he was just going to do it a little while longer. I said, "You do know you can go to jail for that!" Mark replied, "I am incredibly careful, do not worry." We were almost to my aunt's house. He said, "Wait a minute," and hugged and kissed me. He told me how much he loved me and said I was his number one, no matter what. He took my hand and held it the rest of the way.

We arrived at the house. It smelled like fried chicken. We said "Hi" to my aunt Annette and sat in the living room. My aunt was a jokester. She said, "Thank God! I knew you were bringing your better half. I hope he can eat!" We laughed and said, "He isn't 6-feet tall and wearing a size 12 shoe for nothing." She laughed and said, "It must all go to his full lips." He chuckled because he had big lips and was dark skinned.

She went back to the kitchen and finished cooking. The girls came in from the back yard where they were playing ball and jump rope. I told them to go wash up for dinner. They were respectful kids; you could tell by their mannerisms that they were raised with love and respect. I told Mark it was my weekend to visit my mom and I was not looking forward to it. Thank God I must work all afternoon on Saturday. He reassured me that it would be ok.

My aunt came into the living room and told me to follow her. She had something for me. I looked at her oddly. She hugged me tightly and said, "I love you and you are beautiful." That hug meant everything to me; she was instilling love and trust in me. She said Cousin Don would be home any minute and told us to wash our hands one at a time. I went first.

We watched cartoons with the girls until we got called to the table. My aunt added a folded out mental chair for me to sit in. My cousin came in from work and kissed his wife and girls. He gave me and Mark a fist bump and a hug. We sat at the table with fried chicken, baked mac and cheese and string beans with bacon. Everything was plated by my aunt. She put the baby in the highchair. My oldest cousin said grace. I was new to this. She said, "God is good, God is great. Thank you for our food," and we all said, "Amen." We all began to eat.

There was little talk at the table because we were all busy eating the delicious meal my aunt had prepared. After dinner, Mark helped me clean the kitchen. It was easy. He washed the dishes, and I dried them and put them away. My oldest cousin cleaned the table and put away the extra chair. When we were all finished, my aunt said, "That's teamwork! Ya'll know how to put a smile on my face." I said, "You're welcome." Mark said, "Thank you for having me; the food was outstanding." With his lips still greasy from the chicken, he licked his lips. My aunt said, "Your lips speak for it all! I know you enjoyed it. You're welcome, any time."

Mark told me had to get going so I walked him out. I walked him to the porch and gave him a hug and a kiss. He told me not to stress about going to my mom's for the weekend. I then said, "Okay love, I won't." I walked back inside. We all sat around and talked about me going to my mom's house after school. My aunt and cousin said, "Remember you are loved" and told me to respect my mom and dad. I replied with, "I will do my best, but honestly, I do not want to go because I know it will be the same."

My aunt reminded me of my OBGYN appointment on Monday afternoon. She asked me if I was nervous. I was nervous. She asked if I wanted her to come with me to the clinic. I said, "Yes, please, that would be great if you did." Having her support made me feel so much better.

I asked to be excused and went upstairs to my room. I packed my bag for the weekend with my clothes, personal hygiene items, and my uniform for work Saturday. I then showered and laid down until I fell asleep.

Girl from the Wrong Side of the Tracks

Weekend Visits and Work Life

The morning came and I got ready for school. It was going to be 80 degrees; we were in the month of June. I was thinking about graduating eighth grade in just a few weeks. I waited for Donna to pick me up for school. I quickly ate a strawberry Pop-tart; a straight sugar rush is just what I needed in the morning. Donna knocked at my door. I said goodbye to everyone and walked out the door.

As we walked, I asked Donna what she thought about graduation. She said, "to be honest, I was going to ditch it." I asked her why. She said, "I'm going to a hotel party instead of graduation." Donna then asked me what my plans were. I said, "Well to be honest, I do not want to go. It's corny." She invited me to the hotel party. I agreed to go with her. "I don't want to let my mom and dad watch me get a piece of paper." Donna said, "We're going to a hotel party, whoop!!" We both laughed as we walked into school. She went her way, and I went my way.

Homeroom was always fun. Everyone was joking and all wound up because we were about ready to get out of school. The school day was just a half day; it went by fast; we did not do much but laugh, crack jokes and threw out all the year's papers. Donna and I walked home together. It sure was hot and steamy walking up the hill to get home.

All the flowers were in bloom, the trees were green, some had white flowers. Donna and I were excited about the half day. As we walked, I said, "I won't be able to hang out this weekend, I'm going to my mom's." Donna said, "Oh Lord, I know how much you are looking forward to that." I said, "Yeah it shouldn't be that bad. See me Saturday at work. I will be at Burger King. She said, "OK, I will definitely stop down for some food." When I got home, Donna walked one more unit away.

I walked into the house where my aunt was with her arms outstretched. She said, "Lexi, (my nick name), come give me a hug! She squeezed me so tight. She said, "I love you and I just want you to know that you are loved!" I said, "Thank you, Aunty, for being the most positive person in my life. I love you." Then I went to get my bags and told her I would see her on Sunday. I got my bike and headed to my mom's house. It was about a fifteen-to-twenty-minute ride.

I arrived at my mom's house and carried my bike up one flight of stairs. The bike was not too heavy to carry. I used my key to get into the apartment and walked my bike in and said hello to my cousin who was in the kitchen. I walked to my room and put my bags down. The room was nice and clean. My cat, Misty, was lying on my bed so I sat down on the bed and started to pet her.

I looked over at my sister and asked her how everything was going. She replied, "Things are good. We miss you." I said, "I miss you too." My mom and dad were both at work and I heard my brother playing music in his room. I did not go to his room to say hello. I just basically spent the day lying in bed under the fan because it was hot.

An hour before my mom got home, I called her at work to say hello. I asked her what she wanted me to do with the ground beef on the counter. She said, "You can make spaghetti and garlic bread." I said, "Okay, I will start it now." We hung up. We didn't tell each other we loved each other, just "see you when I get home." I cut up an onion and green pepper. I used some garlic powder, onion powder and seasoning salt on the ground beef and vegetables and fried it until it was done.

I drained the meat so the grease would not be in the sauce. Then I put a jar of pasta sauce in the pan and added the meat. I was also boiling water for the pasta. I added one and a half boxes to the boiling water and when that was done, I drained it and ran it under chilly water. I preheated the oven to 350 degrees for the garlic bread. I used the fresh loaf of French bread, sliced it and used butter, garlic powder and parsley flakes.

When my mom came in, she thanked me, sat down in the living room and smoked a cigarette (I hated the smell of cigarettes, but both my mom and dad smoked). My dad came in and said, "Hi, Lexi." I said, "Hi dad, how are you?" He said, "Good, how about you?" I then said, "I am doing good. Dinner is almost ready." He walked down the hall and got his things to shower. I asked my mom if I could put the bread in, but she told me to wait a few minutes so my dad could shower.

I agreed and sat down on the couch and watched tv in the living room. Oprah Winfrey was on the TV. My dad got out of the shower, got dressed and came into the living room, then sat down on the couch. My mom then went into the kitchen and baked the bread. I asked her if she wanted me to set the table. She said, "Sure, that would be a significant help. Thank you." I thought to myself, "Wow, my mom is being kind." I went into the kitchen and set the table.

I put out the forks, knives, and cups. We all made our own plates. Mom called my sister, cousin, brother and dad to the kitchen. We all knew to grab paper plates and a plastic holder. It was quite different at my mom's house; dinner was like an assembly line. We all made our plates and made our way to the dining area, which was not that big, but we made it work.

We were all eating, and dad said, "Excellent job on the sauce, Lexi." I said, "Thank you. It was easy." There was not much conversation at the table because everyone was busy eating. We finished dinner and my cousin cleaned up the kitchen. I went to my room and listened to music on my radio. After my cousin got done with the dishes, she came in and asked me how work was going. I said, "Good. Making money. I have to work tomorrow."

Girl from the Wrong Side of the Tracks

She then said, "I could never work at a fast-food restaurant!" I said to her, "Yeah, you're too good for that. That is why you do not have money and have no job."

We got into an argument. My mom heard us and yelled, "Knock that shit off! I do not want to hear that shit! Stop starting shit, Alexis! My cousin told my mom I was bragging. My mom then said, "That is your problem, Alexis. You always think you're better than someone." I told myself to leave it alone because I learned a long time ago, I will never be right in my mom's eyes. She will always take up for everyone else but me. I just laid on the bed and did not say a word to anyone for the rest of the night. I went to bed early because I had to be up early for work on Saturday.

I got up early and showered. Everyone, except for my mom, was sleeping. I put my uniform on, grabbed my backpack, and went into the living room. I did not bother to eat because I was not hungry. I said, "Good morning" to my mom. She replied, "Morning." I told her my work hours and she told me to be home by nine o'clock. I said, "Okay," and wheeled my bike out the door. I carried it down the flight of stairs and then opened the door to go outside. I held it with my left hand and wheeled the bike out with my right hand while using my body to hold the door as I walked through it. Down a short flight of stairs, I carried my bike to the ground, and I was off to ride to Thames Street.

I traveled down Third Street, the point section in Newport. I hit America's Cup Ave, one of the main streets in downtown, and then I took a left near the Newport Fire Station on West Marlborough Street in Newport, RI. I turned right on Thames, which was a one-way cobblestone road. I always followed traffic laws and rode with traffic. I got to work and locked my bike up to the black pole out front. I put the lock through the tire and the frame. I walked in, put my backpack on the coat rack in the back, and said good morning to my co-workers and manager. Everyone said good morning. I washed my hands and punched in on time. I had to work at the register, take orders and hand out food.

The morning shift turned into a lunch rush and a lot of locals and tourists came in the store. You could hear the frying machines and the microwaves beeping and smell fries, burgers and onions. The food is always fresh for the lunch rush. My co-worker and I did well. We didn't make any mistakes!

Donna came in around 1pm. I took her order. She asked, "Is it your break?" I said, "Yes, right after I give you your food." I finished her order and asked to take my break. My manager said yes. I washed my hands and made my Whopper with cheese, got a large fry, and a medium Sprite. Donna and I walked up to the second floor. This Burger King had three floors! We sat at a table, ate our food, and had some small talk. She reminded me the party was in a week. I said, "I know. I cannot wait!" We finished our meal, emptied our trash, and walked downstairs. She said, "Bye! I will see you Monday." I said, "Okay sounds good." The shift flew by and before I knew it, it was time to go home.

Acting Grown

I got my things and rode back to my mom's house. Everyone was in their rooms. I put my bag down and grabbed a towel to wash the Burger King smell off me. After my shower, I laid in my bed with the TV on until I fell asleep. The next day, which was Sunday, I could leave at any time. I chose to leave first thing in the morning. I needed the positivity from my aunt. I said bye to mom, dad, sister, brother and cousin and was off to my aunt's house.

I arrived and there was nothing but hugs from the kids, my aunt, and my cousin Don. They asked about my weekend. I told them it was fine. I was not up for sharing the negativity of the weekend. We had a nice Sunday afternoon and got ready for Monday and Tuesday, our last days of school.

My aunt went with me to the clinic that Monday. I was so scared. They told me they needed a urine sample when I got there. That was pretty easy. Then, she said they needed to exam. I felt like I was being fondled by a strange woman. Then they had me lay on a table with tissue paper. She gave me directions to scoot down, and put my legs in the stirrups, and spread my legs. They draped another tissue paper on my lap and had me spread my legs.

It was awkward and cold. The doctor stated that they were going to begin the examination. She said I would feel a cold jelly and that would be her feeling for my uterus. Then she went on to say that she would insert a tool to help her with examination. It hurt and I felt a lot of pressure down there. Then she used another tool, which she described as a brush, to get a sample of my cervix. That really was painful and uncomfortable. Once she was done, she told me I could get dressed.

I wondered why my mom would make me do this to get on birth control. There had to be an easier way. I went back into the waiting room where my aunt was waiting for me. We got the results of the urine test; I was not pregnant, which I already knew, but you never know because Mark and I continued to have unprotected sex. So, in my mind, I dodged a bullet. I was not ready to be nobody's mom. My aunt went over to the basket on the table and gave me a hand full of condoms.

I laughed and she told me to protect myself. The doctor came to explain the birth control. I was to start the same day when I got my menstrual cycle. I already made up my mind that I was not taking the pills. I just went to shut my mother up. The clinic was across the street from my aunt's house, so we walked home. She gave me the birds and the bees spiel. I just laughed. She asked, "What's so funny?" I just said, "You! I appreciate it. This is something my own parents did not take the time to do."

The next day was our last day of school. I had thrown out all the tickets and home notices of the graduation. It was all set. Donna and I were not going. We had a party to attend that week. Donna and I walked to school talking about how we couldn't believe we would be in high school that upcoming September. We agreed it was surreal.

I saw Mark this morning because he made it a point to come see me. He asked me about my weekend and my appointment. I told him how things were at my mom's house and told him all about the doctor. His response was, "Don't sweat things at your mom's house. Ignore all the petty things. I'm glad you had a good appointment at the clinic." He asked me if I was going to take the birth control. I said, "No, why? What do you think?" He stated that it was up to me because it's my body. I said, "You know that we have to be careful because I could get pregnant."

In a joking manner he said it would be a blessing from God, but we don't need a baby right now. I agreed. The bell rang for class so off we went to our homerooms. The day went superfast. There was nothing to do. We just talked in each class and signed yearbooks.

I went to Mark's house after school. We walked to his house together. Nobody was home, which was the normal thing for his house. You know what we did. He put on some music. We acted grown and had unprotected sex for hours on end. It was like he fed my passion for sex, which was not done with anyone else but him. It was always sensual, steamy, and passionate.

After we were done, I went downstairs and made some fried chicken and pasta alfredo. We both ate. Then we took a shower together, which led to more sex. He bent me over while I was standing with one knee on the tub to steady myself. I wasn't expecting that, but you never knew with Mark. After that episode, we finally washed each other up. That act was more sensual than I could imagine. It was like being at one with another soul. We washed each other's bodies and explored at the same time.

Finally, we were all done with the shower. We got dressed. I told him I had to get going because I was late for dinner. He said he would drive me so I would only be late by a few minutes. I agreed and off we went to my aunt's house. He was driving illegally because he didn't have his license yet but had a car and a moped. The life of a drug dealer! He didn't stay; he just dropped me off.

I told him I would call him in a couple of hours. I walked into the house, and everyone was at the table.

I explained to my aunt that I was late because I had cooked dinner for Mark and me. She said it was okay and to just call next time I was going to be late or eat out. I said, "Okay, sounds good." My aunt and cousin were very flexible unlike my mom.

Graduation day finally arrived. I got dressed up in a silk outfit. It was an all-red button-down shirt with a collar, silk shorts, and red leather shoes. Yes, at a young age I had the real deal because Mark made sure of that; he spoiled me.

I phoned Donna after getting dressed. I asked her what time the party started. She said, "Whatever time we get there." I told her I was ready. She was too. I said, "Come over and we can call a cab." I told her to call the cab to her house and I'd be picked up at the top of Chapel Street. She said, "Okay, sounds good." I told my aunt I wouldn't be home for dinner and asked if my curfew was still 9pm. She said it was ok and extended my curfew to 11pm since school was done. I smiled and thought to myself, "Word up!" (meaning, yes!) I walked up the street. Donna stopped the cab to pick me up. We got to the hotel, which was Pineapple Inn. You could tell by the outside setup it was a low budget hotel. It was white and all the rooms were connected. There had to be about 40 rooms in total, maybe a little more. There were rooms across the street from one another with a parking lot separating them and a small section that was connected to the adjacent buildings that said, "Office."

We knocked on the door, and they let us in. The room was filled with a mix of cigarettes and weed. There was enough liquor for an army. They had just ordered pizza. There were about twelve of us in the room when the pizza came. My friend told us to make ourselves comfortable. I made a drink with vodka and cranberry juice. Donna had a beer. We sat down, mingled with all the drug dealers and their girlfriends. They had music going through the TV. I didn't know who the artists were because I didn't particularly like rap music. I called Mark on the phone to let him know where I was. He reminded me that graduation was in a couple of hours. I said, "I know. I'm not going." He said, "Why?" He tried to convince me to go, but I told him I wasn't going and would be at the party.

We hung up the phone and I went back to mingling and laughing. Soon enough, the room really got packed. There was just standing room only. We were packed like sardines. After a few hours, Mark arrived. Everyone was high fiving him. He gave me a hug and a kiss and whispered in my ear, "I walked the stage for us, baby." I then whispered back, "Thank you, baby." We ate pizza, but after a few minutes Mark says to me,
"I want Chinese food." Then he yelled, "Aye yo, aye yo! Who wants Chinese food?" Everyone was down, meaning they wanted Chinese food.

All the guys went to their cars. They went and picked up all kinds of Chinese food. They came back with so many brown bags of food it wasn't even funny. When the smokers smoke weed, they get the munchies. It was a good time. I asked Mark to bring me home around 10pm. He did and then he said he was going back to the party. I said, "Okay, Donna stayed." It was like I was an adult acting like an adult, but I was a young, teenage girl who grew up too fast.

Girl from the Wrong Side of the Tracks

It was like living two lives while growing up. I had school, home life with my aunt, chores and then every other weekend I went to my grandmother's and grandfather's. My life was always split up. I really had to switch mind sets when I did things. I have to say, I did it well for many years.

Setbacks and New Beginnings

In September 1990, we started high school. We rode the city bus to school because regulations stated that our address was too close for us to ride a school bus. Donna and her sister and a few other girls from Chapel Terrace rode the same bus. It was like three weeks into the school year when Mark and a few others were raided for drugs. I found out through word of mouth during the school day. I ditched school and went to the courthouse. This time they got him on three delivery charges of crack cocaine, possession of crack cocaine, and $3,500 in cash. I cried while they read off the charges.

They remanded him to the training school. I lost my love and best friend. They kept him for two years. During those two years, I received letters in the mail and phone calls. During those two years, I was reunified with my mother and continued to work at Burger King. I also babysat in my spare time.

In 1992, Mark was released from training school. We continued to be together. There were still issues of him cheating on me with other girls, but I still stayed by his side. He went back to hustling drugs upon his release and went to school. We were now in the tenth grade and still had unprotected sex. In the eleventh grade, I got pregnant and faced parenthood.

I was in denial for a few months. I had a problem at six months pregnant. He gave me a STD called Trichomonas which was Vaginitis, a STD from having multiple sex partners and not being clean. I cried because I was leaking fluid, and my baby could've been born early. The doctor prescribed me a pill which cost about $400.00. My insurance didn't cover it. I called him and told him what was going on. He agreed to pick up the pill at the pharmacy. He pulled up in his car with his new girlfriend, an older woman.

At this point, I was sure we were over. He brought up the pill. I thanked him. He did not do much to help prepare for our son. He ended up going back to training school before the birth of our child, and rumor had it that Lauren was pregnant by him too. Mark denied it. He said it was Jayceon's and that she slept with the whole football team.

My mom helped me prepare for the baby. She stated, "You will finish high school and I will keep him while you're in school." I thought to myself, "Wow, thank you because I do not know anything about being a mother." Mark was picked up again on drug charges with his girlfriend. They sentenced him to a year this time. I was so full of emotions. I knew in my heart that I loved him. My mom did not say it, but she did not like him. I was so torn at times all I could do was cry. I did this mostly in the shower.

Girl from the Wrong Side of the Tracks

Time passed. I got letters and phone calls again from him. I was on a waiting list for public housing. I finished the 11th grade. I ended early because I was due to have my baby on June 11. I went into labor on that day exactly. My water broke in my sleep. I woke up and told my mom. She took me to the hospital. I had really sharp contractions. The staff would come to see if I was making progress with my labor. This was the course over several hours. I was so tired. My dad and biological father were there. My mom didn't leave my side.

I was in labor all day. I chose my biological father to be with me for the C-section. I sent my mom and dad home. I don't remember why I chose him to be there with me. I don't remember much about the C-section either because I was on pain meds. When I woke up, the nurse was wiping me down with a warm cloth. She was giving me a sponge bath! "Where is my baby?" I asked. She said, "I'll take you to him shortly." I was so excited to finally meet my baby boy.

When my dad gave him to me, I was in pure love; tears ran down my face. He was so perfect and cute. His dad called me on the phone and asked me how I was feeling. I told him I was sore and had to have a C-section. He said he knew because called the hospital and spoke to my mom. All he could say was that he would be home in one more month. He said he loved me and asked what I named our son. I said, "His name is Jahmere." He told me that once he came home, he would sign his birth certificate so he could carry his last name. I agreed. He stated that he wanted to move in with me and Jahmere. I said, "Yes, I would love our little family to be together."

After staying with my mom for about 3 weeks, I was ready to be on my own and in my own apartment with him. I had an infection when I was in the hospital though. She brought him home while I healed and got better. It was just a few days before I was able to go home.

Mark and I lived in a one-bedroom apartment with Jahmere. It seemed to be perfect, but some things remained the same. Mark continued to sell drugs. I told him to stop, but he didn't listen. I said, "No drugs in the house." He had people coming to the house to buy drugs. He had me selling drugs to his family and people he knew for a long time. I knew this was risky and I was scared, but this is the way he wanted it, so I complied with his wishes. I was an "at home dealer" selling crack cocaine.

Mark would take our son on daily walks for hours. I thought he was taking him to his aunt's house. He was, she lived up the street from us in another run-down housing place called Tonomy Hill. This was a major housing complex for low-income families. There was crime and it was loaded with drugs and a gang they called "Hillside Posse." I don't believe Mark was a part of this gang, but who knows? I didn't know everything about what he did when he was out. He kept me in the house except for school and work. It was like I was a prisoner of love.

My mom told me one day that he was selling crack from the baby carriage and baby bag. I asked him and he denied it. I told him he better not be. My mom said she heard it from a friend who said the police were watching him. All summer he did this activity. I went out with him to his aunt's house a couple of times. He bought an old silver Cadillac for us to get around town. It was a fixer upper. He put a sound system in and had other work done on it all the time by a street mechanic who was a customer of his. Then he bought an older yellow Cadillac. I ended up crashing into a pole early one morning because the brakes failed. I didn't get hurt in the crash, but we needed a new, safer car.

Mark had the money. We tried dealerships, but both of our credit reports were "ghosts" as they explained. We had to apply for a gas card to start a credit history. I applied for a Shell gas station card. I got approved and I began to make charges and payments. Mark went to the car auction and bought me a red Volkswagen GTI. It was small and sporty. I loved it. It had a gray interior and the back seats folded down. I registered it in my name just in case he got in trouble with the police.

One day, he came home with a handgun. I asked what it was for. He said, "Your protection." I said to him, "I don't want that here in this house." He said, "Don't worry, I'll put it right here in the arm of the chair." I was terrified of the gun. After that day, I never looked for it again. I pretended it wasn't there. He would take trips to the city, which took forever because it was New York City.

I don't remember where in New York. I only went once, and it was to a white brick house in what I would describe as a "ghetto." There were shoes hanging from the telephone poles, boarded up houses and windows, and trash everywhere you looked. Not to mention the addicts and homeless roaming on the streets. I never took another ride again because he had me hold on to the brick of cocaine! When we got there, he cooked it up to make crack.

We would go to school each day and my mom would pick up my son each morning and then bring him home in the afternoons.

One fall afternoon, Mark brought home two guys I had never met before. We greeted each other. I took the baby into the room while they talked. He was selling guns to them. I asked him who they were. He said, "Two friends of mine that live down the street here in our complex." As time passed, we continued the same behavior. I knew in my heart it was only a matter of time before he got locked up again.

Dealing Drugs Gets You Nowhere

One night my sister and her friend asked to spend the night. I agreed. That night I was woken up by guns drawn on me and Mark! It was the Feds! They took him out before I could say anything. We were butt naked in my heated waterbed in the dead of winter. They asked me who I was. I told them. They had me get dressed. Then, they handcuffed me and sat me down in the kitchen chair. My sister was in the living room handcuffed with her friend. They said, "We have a search warrant for this house." I said, "OK, there are no drugs here." They brought in the dogs and did a manual search.

The dogs were sniffing the baby's crib. They took apart the crib and found a baggy full of crack cocaine! I was shocked that he would tie crack to our baby's crib. They let me make a call to my mom so she could pick up my son and sister. Her friend had to call her mom. They took me to the police station and booked me for the drugs and intent to deliver. I got out of jail after going to court. I was in front of the judge pleading not guilty. I was released on personal recognizance and Mark was not allowed on the property. I had to fight for my housing. I had help from Legal Services to fight my housing eviction. Mark called me and said he signed a statement saying the drugs were his. It was only right of him after I went to jail and was fighting housing.

I went to visit him. He told me not to worry, all his runners (smaller drug dealers) would take care of me. He asked me if they tore up the carpet and I said no. He said there were drugs under the carpet and in the hallway. Once I got home, I found them, and I flushed them all.

I was done with selling drugs and that lifestyle. I had a child to think of. Mark would call every day, sometimes several times a day. One day, he started to tell me what they put in his discovery packet (all the information due to the arrest). He stated that they got him on a delivery and gun charges. I asked, "With who?" He said, "It was the two guys that were in our house that day, the house I used to hang out at." I said, "Those guys were police informants and you got caught up with them! I warned you about them! How do two guys get an apartment in low-income housing with no family? So much for outsmarting the police!"

I had my day again in court on the drugs charges. They dismissed all charges because of the statement Mark wrote. They did not want me. They had been gunning for him since he was a juvenile. I was charged with maintaining a narcotic nuance.

After 2 months of fighting the eviction, I signed a paper with Legal Aid saying that no one else, including Mark, would live in the residence for a period of one year. Not only did I get to keep my apartment, but I also moved to a two-bedroom apartment. I met four new friends. They were our neighbors. Our kids played in the hallway on the third floor. We would go to each other's houses. I still would spend time in the Tonomy Hill projects at Mark's aunt's house. I would also receive drug money from the runners that ran drugs for him. It helped me financially to take care of our needs.

I caught him by surprise at one of the visits. I went through the checkpoint, entered the visiting room and saw him sitting there holding hands with another girl! When I approached the table, the girl stood up, said nothing, and left. We had an issue and something to talk about. I asked who she was but all he would say is, "my friend." I said, "You looked like more than friends when you were holding hands." He fed me lies on top of lies and wouldn't tell me her name. I was pissed off to see another woman there after I had been through all this with him and still stayed by him. This time I stayed for the sake of my son. I told him I wasn't going to visit for a while because he was cheating on me even while in prison. He said he was just using them for money. I said, "Oh like me? You used me too. I put money in your account. I make every visit I can, and this is the way I get paid back! I'm so tired of your lies and bullshit. You are unbelievable!" Then I got up from the table and walked out of the visiting room. I buckled my son in his car seat for the 45-minute drive back to Newport, RI from Cranston, RI. I cried all the way home, wiping tears away as I drove.

In my senior year, I met a fellow student that I had grown fond of. He would come over and hang out. As time passed by, we became more than friends; we became intimate. No one knew except my friend in the basement apartment. It's like we had a code. We called them "creepers," meaning lovers on the down low. We continued this relationship for a long time.

I still visited Mark from time to time. He let me know he was close to work release, and he would be working at a warehouse to start, then get a job locally in a restaurant. I would visit the job site, bring him lunch, and then we would have sex in a part of the warehouse that had a makeshift bedroom. It had a bed, a nightstand, a radio and candles. I was not fond of having sex there, but again, it's what he wanted. In hindsight, he had me brainwashed. I did whatever he wanted me to do. I had missed a period and was nervous that I was pregnant again.

I called my doctor and took a test. It came back positive. My doctor scheduled an ultrasound. I was six weeks pregnant. I showed him the ultrasound. He was so happy. I was not. I couldn't believe that I was on baby number two and Jahmere and the baby would be two and a half years apart.

I graduated high school in 1994. I had a tough pregnancy. Mark was released from prison. He lived with me for some of the pregnancy and then he got his own apartment in downtown Newport, right next door to his job. He and his cousin shared this apartment. I knew it was only a matter of time before he would begin to cheat on me again.

One night we had an argument at my apartment because he wanted me to give him my car. I refused so he slashed all the tires and keyed the car. He also threw a vacuum at me while I was 7 months pregnant. I blocked it by shutting the door quickly or it would have hit me in the stomach. This is the first time he tried to hurt me physically.

I called the police, and he was arrested on a domestic assault; I was so scared that he did this to me. I found out that he was back dating Kathy. I felt like I was used. He kept going back and forth with me and this circle of girls. Who knows how many other women I did not know about. He began to stalk me at my job and at home, flashing headlights and flashing lights into my apartment window. He knew the baby was going to be born in February; it was a planned C-section. He said he would be there; the time came for me to go into the hospital.

He was not there; it was my mom and my friend. This time the delivery was much smoother.

It was a boy. I wanted to name him Isaiah. I signed the birth certificate. Visitors came and went all day, still no Mark until later that night. He asked me if Kathy could come in. I said, "Hell no! Your girlfriend does not need to see my baby." He came in with the gift of fingernail clippers and a pacifier. All he could say was he forgot about the time and that he heard I had the baby, so he came to the hospital.

The only thing Mark wanted from me was sex and in that hospital room that is exactly what he got; he did not care that I had an operation to have his baby. He just wanted to fulfill his twisted ways of sex. All I could think of during this act was getting caught by a nurse. I felt awful. This was not how I imagined the birth of our second son. He took the birth certificate, signed his name, and filled in the name, which was not Isaiah. He named him after himself. I was so mad when I saw the name in the baby's cradle. There was nothing I could do about it unless we went to court.

My mom was livid! She thought I did it. I explained what had happened. I went home two days later, and he was in my apartment with that whole lie "I want to be a family; I want to be here for my kids and you." That didn't last exceptionally long because he couldn't be faithful. We split once again. He would come take Jahmere out for the day or sometimes overnight, but never little Mark. I always questioned why he wouldn't take both.

I concluded that he wanted me tied down with one of our children and in the house. We went back and forth that year.

Abuse and How It Changed Me

When little Mark was 6 months old, Mark found a phone number in my coat pocket for a male friend who I hadn't seen in a while. My friend gave me his number and we planned to go out and play pool together, just good, clean fun. Mark made me take off all my clothes and get into my bedroom closet. He held me at gunpoint and said, "If I can't have you, nobody will."

I tried to tell him the guy was just a friend, but he kept yelling. The more he yelled, the closer he got to me in the closet. Tears were running down my face. He put the gun in my mouth and said, "Give me a reason why I shouldn't blow your head off." I sobbed and sobbed. I said, "I love you and our kids! Please don't hurt me." After an hour or two of keeping me in the closet, he let me go. I didn't call the police out of fear for me and my children, but I knew I had to get away from his madness. That evening, I called my cousins in California and told them I needed to get away for a while. They were more than glad to help me out during this crazy time in my life.

My cousin looked up a round-trip flight from Rhode Island to San Diego, California. I had plans to take baby Mark, but Jahmere was going to stay back with my mother. I had to move things out, like clothes and toys, in huge laundry bags because he was still stalking me. I brought things to my mother's house. I was leaving my apartment, our furniture and the life I knew behind. My life and my children's lives mean more to me than materialistic possessions.

One evening everything was all set and I drove me and the kids to my mother's house. I borrowed luggage from my dad and packed all mine and baby Mark's things. I was slated to leave that next morning. I had no time for goodbyes. The only people that knew we were leaving were my son Jahmere, my mom, and my dad. My return date was up in the air.

That next morning, I was so nervous. I had never flown on an airplane. I had a special harness for baby Mark because he couldn't walk at the time. We had a layover in Chicago O'Hare airport. My mom was driving us to the airport. I said, "I'll see you soon," to Jahmere. "Mommy will be back." He was too young to really understand. He was comfortable with my mom. I checked in the luggage and quickly after that we were on an airplane headed for San Diego, California. On the plane Mark had a really bad bowel movement. It was all over him. Thank God I packed an extra set of clothes. The bathroom was so small. I was a big girl trying to wash my baby in the sink. I made it work somehow and we went back to be seated.

I knew the guy next to me was annoyed with having to sit in the same row as us. Mark cried at times. It was a long flight. I believe it was a total of six hours, counting the layover. We made it to the airport in California. It was big! My cousin was there to greet us. We went in her car and drove to her house. It was a far drive. So many miles of highway and traffic like I'd never seen before. This was a big city.

We got to her house. My older cousin lived there too, which was unknown to me. There was also a guy roommate. Over the next couple of days, I found out it was a party house, not really what I wanted for me and my son. They were friends with men in the Navy. They were all nice to me and my son, but still it was a huge change. It seemed like every night the men from the ship came over and brought drinks. This was a drastic change for me.

I had to engage with strangers. I did drink sometimes to be social, but it was very different for me at night. I had to lie down on the couch with my son with people laughing and drunk. It turned into a big slumber party.

When we got there, we went food shopping and I spent most of my cash. The plan was for me to get public assistance. The wait was so long for an appointment. I stopped spending money and putting it in the house because they fed everyone, and others would drink the juice and eat the snacks.

I would go out each day to the gas station and buy milk and single serve cereal, juice, and banana for my son. For lunch and dinner, we ate out. I would call my mom every day and talk to Jahmere and my mom. I was homesick after the first week, but I knew I didn't move there for nothing.

The weather was depressing. It would be 90 degrees every day, no rain. I was used to seeing the water in the summertime. My cousin took me to the WIC office where they provide lower income people with children with formula, milk, eggs, cheese, juice, and cereal. I was accepted and began to use the checks for my son and asked that no one touch those items.

For the most part, they respected my son's food. I began to look for apartments, but the areas that I could afford were very slummy and dangerous. I continued to stay with my cousin, but as time passed, I knew that I didn't want to be there. One day, while I was in the shower, a man came into the bathroom while I was in a towel. I said, "Get out! I'm trying to get dressed." He said, "Wait a minute. I want to let you know I like you and I want you to be my girlfriend." I said, "No thank you. I am not interested. Now please get out of the bathroom." He left. I hurried up and got dressed. I felt so uncomfortable that someone would just walk into the bathroom when someone was in it with the door closed. There wasn't a lock on the door, we all just knew if the door was shut, someone was in there.

After that, I went into the living room and said I was going out.

I took my son for a walk. The closest thing to the apartment was the gas station and a taco shop. I bought him some snacks and a burrito to share. When we got back to the apartment, they were smoking weed. Little Mark and I sat outside on the porch and ate our food.

We sat outside on the concrete stairs, no grass, just the sound of music coming from the house. I placed a phone call to my mom telling her I wanted to come home. She said to just wait a little while and see how it goes. I explained how homesick I was. She reassured me that it would be ok. We ended the call with "I love you" and she said she would send pictures. I said,
"OK."

We went inside and just sat on the couch. The music was playing, the TV was on, and everyone else was just sitting around. The next day, my cousin answered the phone and someone on the other end asked for me. I got on the phone and said, "Hello?" I got no response after saying it three times, so I hung up the phone. I didn't think much about it because who besides a professional person from California knew I was there?

It happened again but this time he spoke and said, "I know you're there. Don't think I won't find you." It was Mark! I called my mom immediately and told her what happened. She said she knew because he went to the daycare trying to get my son and my mom was called. The teacher told him I had moved to California. Not much happened. My son still went to school. I had given my mom guardianship in case anything was to happen to me. She filed a no contact order on my son's behalf. I told her I was setting up my flight to come back home. The plan was for me to stay with her. I flew out with my baby several days later, on the red eye flight so we could sleep and get a direct flight to Warwick, RI. The flight went smoothly. I got food from the taco shop because it was very good. Those burritos were like a taste of heaven in your mouth. Little Mark slept well on the plane.

We got there around 8am. My mom picked us up. We got our luggage and packed it in the car. I gave my son a big hug and kiss and told him how much I missed him. It seemed like forever, but it was only 7 weeks. We arrived home only to hear that Mark and one of his new girlfriends had been in a car accident. He went through the windshield. He was pretty banged up, but ok. I started going to church with my stepmother, Nicole. We went every Sunday and during the week. A woman called me from me from my seat and said, "I know there is something on your heart and God is ready to fix it. All you got to do is say it." So, I said to her, "I want my son's father removed from my life. I don't want to fight or be chased. I just want to be free." She said, "You shall be in Jesus' name, amen."

She laid her hands on me, putting her hands on my head and shoulders gently. I was weeping when I sat down in my seat. The whole church was praying and speaking in tongues. After church, I went home and felt the weight of the world had been lifted off my shoulders.

About a month had passed. I had applied for housing in Tonomy Hill. I went to the mall one day with little Mark and we ran into his father. I was so scared! He approached us and just picked him up and kissed him. He said nothing to me. We walked away and went into the store. That was the last time I saw him. I had gone to court to legally change little Mark's name; I made his middle name his first name and gave him a new middle name. I didn't want him to carry his father's first name and for him to be a junior. I ended up making the right choice because we moved out of my mother's house to Tonomy Hill, me and both of my children.

Mark called me on my birthday to wish me a "Happy Birthday." He asked me if he could buy the boys new beds. I said, "No, they have everything they need." Then, he asked if he could come over. I didn't even know he knew where I lived.

Placing Blame

Two weeks after my birthday, I was with the church sisters. I don't know how I didn't hear it on the morning news, probably because I was surrounded by love all day. One of the church sisters braided my hair. I had to take the baby to speech class.

After leaving speech class, a friend walked up to me and asked me if I heard about Mark. I said, "He is always doing something. I really don't care to hear about it." She said, "No, he is dead. He got shot."

I walked away, put the baby in the car seat, and I drove home. It was April so I drove with the windows down. Another friend stopped me and asked me the same question. I flipped and said, "If you don't stop asking me if I'm ok, I will fuck you up!" I went into the house and put on the news to see if there was any truth behind what they were saying. Soon after, my church sister and my mom arrived. Then, the segment came on that Mark was shot and killed in a Mc Donald's robbery. I cried and uttered the words, "Now my kids won't have a father."

My church sisters began to pray. My mom just watched on. I told them I would be ok. I still had doubt in my mind, so I said I would be right back. I drove down the street to his aunt's house asking them if it was true. They said, "Yes, it's true he really is gone." They hugged me. I got back in my car and went home. Food was being sent over from neighbors.

I called his sister's house to ask her about the arrangements. She said they would be made soon but they would be in Connecticut. I didn't hear anything for a few days. I talked to friends. They said they were committing these crimes down south and made their way up east. I wondered why in the world they would do that.

Mark did it with another man that was on the run with a hostage. The Massachusetts police came to my house warning me about this dangerous man and told me to always watch my surroundings. I heeded the warning and locked all my doors. I got a call one Sunday morning from Mark's brother saying that his service was that day, in Connecticut. I got the boys in their suits, and I was already dressed for church. I had only a few minutes to follow his uncle on the highway. We got there and it was a grave site funeral. His mom said nothing to me. She was consoling one of his high school girlfriends. I thought to myself that it was very odd, and I felt like me and my kids were outsiders.

The funeral was over. The pastor said a few words. Mark's mother was the only one who spoke. We got to an aunt's house for the after ceremony and still, nobody talked to me. His mother did not acknowledge my children. The whole time I felt like an outsider, so I got my kids together and found my way back home.

Girl from the Wrong Side of the Tracks

A few days later, his mom called me and blamed me for the death of her son. I said, "Excuse me? Why are you blaming me? I haven't had anything to do with your son." She said, "You chased him to his death." I asked, "How so?" She said, "For money for child support." I said, "You're wrong. There is an order for him to go to court, but the last court date he didn't show for my kids."

Mark had a daughter that was 1-day apart from my oldest child that he denied. He took a DNA test, and it came back 97.8% and my oldest came back 99.9%. He felt some type of way paying child support for a child that was not 99.9% his.

The conversation ended because she hung up on me. We did not even have a proper goodbye because she kept us from the wake. I never really had closure. I knew he was gone but I never got to say goodbye. That still hurts until to this very day. How could his own mother deny me and my children a proper goodbye? It just didn't sit right with my soul that another human being could be so cold and distant towards us and have the nerve to blame me for her son's death. Another man was charged with Mark's death.

In my mind, she couldn't hold me accountable for his life of crime. The man was his partner doing these fast-food heists and finally got caught. He killed him! Put the blame where it belongs. I admit, I carried it with me for years. It came to a point where I had to let it go. It was hard. Many feelings and emotions were attached to this for many years. After his death, I had to bury my emotions.

Life changed for me and my boys. Amir had a speech delay and had behavioral problems. I was always being called by daycare and schools to pick him up for aggressive behavior. He would have severe outbursts on his brother Jahmere and me. He ended up in the Bradley Hospital Pedi-Partial Program. It was a 45-minute ride. Thank goodness my job was flexible, and I worked in the field.

I participated with him two days a week on the floor and watched the staff role play with me and him on how to respond to his outbursts. There were also many times he was hospitalized. Jahmere still spent a lot of time with my mom due to the outbursts and forms of aggression. Jahmere finally ended up moving in with her because I had my hands full. This hurt me deep down to my core. I had to have my mom basically raise my child while I was trying to save another. This went on for many years. I had to leave my job to tend to Amir full time along with an agency that worked with children and their families. I had people working in my home full time.

I had moved twice over the course of this time to a three bedroom. It was much better for my family. I had hopes that Jahmere would come back home to me since he had his own room. It was decorated in sports themed things he loved, but it was too late. He would just come on weekends.

My life did a total 180-degree turn. I met a guy that was a childhood friend of Mark's brother. He was now 21 years old. I had known him for years. When I moved, he began to come over every day to see me. We would have a drink here and there. Then, suddenly, he would bring a guy that he worked with. He was cool. We would all hang out in my house and have drinks. Then I developed a romantic relationship with his friend.

We would have drinks and play cards. It seemed like before I knew it, he was in my bed. I wasn't in a relationship, so I saw no harm in having a strictly sexual relationship. It fed my high sexual drive. He was my "booty call." My friend introduced me to four more guys that lived in the neighborhood. In my eyes, I was becoming popular in my new condo. Little did I know it would lead to something a little bit hectic and crazy.

My newfound popularity turned my house into a party house at night, after work. My friends would not leave until the next day. Angel slept in my bed, Izzy and Elizabeth were dating, and slept in the room meant for Jahmere, and Beats and Rome stayed from time to time. Everyone was from Providence. I don't know how they migrated to Newport. I thought they stayed in an abandoned house or with the neighbor next door because she was an older woman who drank with them nightly and daily too.

She was not fond of our new friendship so she would call the cops often. She said I was giving alcohol to minors, which was not true. They came a few times when there was no music on because she would say I was having a party. The police stopped responding to calls to my house from her. I'm not sure if that's legal or not, but a cop's son did stay with me too.

I began to feed them and buy drinks for everyone because after a while, I noticed they were some broke ass folks just living off me. I allowed it.

Me and Angel started dating. He was the most handsome, green-eyed man I had seen. He worked a lot on computers and music and looked after Amir when I worked at my night job. I was head over heels for him. Back then, we used the beep phones. I got us both phones from Sprint. He was spoiled. I had a credit card for every store in the mall.

We went shopping and got him some new clothes and personal things because I hated seeing him in the same clothes. Little did I know he was sharing with Izzy, his youngest brother. Elizabeth and Nene, a friend of Elizabeth's, were still in high school. They would go sometimes and stay over sometimes. It was like a big frat house after work. Angel would pick me up, sometimes he would say he was stuck at the studio so I would have to call a cab. That just goes to show how naive and trusting I was. I even got him a gas card on my credit account.

Girl from the Wrong Side of the Tracks

I worked two jobs: one during the day and one at night. Money was no issue. You could say I was "hood rich." Everyone wanted to be my friend and come over. I had a nice, fully furnished, 3-bedroom condo. I had nice things. I picked up a third job from time to time. I was a plus size model. It paid good and the perks included discounts on clothes.

Things began to get out of control when we all started going to the bar every night. We met a bartender in one bar whose father owned the bar. We started having after hours parties and charged $20 to get in the door. The fee included 1 cup and food. The police never came. Our friend would bring over crates of liquor and kegs every day. Then, they started smoking weed in my house. I did not like the smell, but I let them do it anyway.

Angel and I had a romantic relationship. I was afraid of losing him if I said no to anything. He introduced me to some of his friends in Providence and across the bridge in North Kingstown, RI. It was fair to say that I was a functional drunk.
I never drank and drove. We lived within walking distance of the two bars we went to.

My mom told me I needed help because she said I had bipolar disorder. She worked for a psychiatrist. I went for an appointment. He asked us a ton of questions about my life, and I answered him. It was almost like a 2-hour appointment. He gave me a ton of prescriptions to fill. I had no idea what they were for because I made half the shit up. I filled them, hid them in my room, and read the precautions. They all said not to drink or be careful if using alcohol. One night I took some and had two beers. I was smashed out of my mind. I liked the way it made me feel. Soon I quit my day job so I could sleep all day after taking the pills. Angel would get Amir ready for school.

I was mixing pills and liquor. When my appointment came around, I would say I was still not feeling better. He gave me stronger drugs. Then, a friend discovered my stash. We would take pills together. I hid my stash again and put a lock on my door because there was always a house full of people.

One night, Angel's phone went off. He left it at home. I read it. It was his ex-girlfriend asking if he was coming back to Providence to stay the night. I confronted him and he said, "That was meant for my friend who she has kids with." I said, "Oh, then why is she texting you?" I played dumb and listened to his story. I was used to being lied to. I took my car key back and took him off my gas card.

We had an on and off sexual relationship, but the sad thing was, I was deeply in love with him. We lived together for a year, partying and going out. Things got so bad, and my house had the reputation of being a party house. My landlord and a detective came by to see me. They asked me if I wanted all of them to go. They told me the story of how they took over another apartment on the property. All I had to do was say I wanted them gone. This was my way out of living in chaos. I told them I wanted them all gone and all their personal belongings. They woke everyone up and told them to vacate the premises. They enacted a no trespass order.

One by one they gathered what they had at my house and left. I asked for my door locks to be changed so I would not come home to a surprise.

Fake Friends & My Downfall

I lived in peace and quiet for a few months. I even had the pastor of the church come cast out all the demons. I stopped drinking and using pills. Life was great. I still was not back to work because I had Amir with his behavioral problems.

I finally got the help I needed which was in home support. They sent a male staff person who developed a great relationship with Amir. It was like he was his big brother and a role model. He set the expectations that I had in place and Amir followed the program. Some days would be difficult but that was to be expected.

Amir joined a martial arts program which he excelled in. On Saturdays he played basketball. I began to see progress in his behaviors, but it was like a full-time job. His staff worked inside my house 35 hours a week, one on one with Amir. We would go see Jahmere several times a week. Their relationship had improved but Jahmere still was not ready to come back home with us. He always had something bigger and better than I could do. For instance, my mom installed an above ground pool. What kid wouldn't want to leave that!?

Every summer since 5th grade, I paid and sent him to summer school. My mom was his caretaker, but I didn't know what she did or did not do with him as far as school was concerned. If it was anything like how she parented me, she didn't go to parent-teacher conferences or check for homework.

He had everything he needed. He received my disability pension. He was in therapy over the things that happened such as why he didn't live with mom and processing the death of his father. He was old enough to understand what we told him.

Several months after everyone left my house, I had Marie come over. She came with a male friend. We all talked. He seemed smart and was into black power. I didn't care for that part of his conversation. He always compared things to old slavery days and why we were wrong in our conversation. I let them stay for dinner. He left around 8pm. Marie and I just listened to music and talked about all the good times we shared. Marie was a close friend that seemed to be a church person. She could quote scripture. She was married. She had given up her apartment, but this was nothing new. She bounced around from house to house and state to state. Her husband had a drug problem and there was chatter in the streets that he also liked men.

Long story short, she ended up moving in with me for several months. She was good at cleaning, cooking, and helping out with Amir, but once again, I took on another responsibility. She had no job. I was always paying her way when we did things. I supported her smoking habit and bought her personal needs products. Don't get me wrong, she was a good friend, but I was getting tired of her male friend spending the night also. She split from her husband because he gave her an STD. I had two people living with me because her friend was homeless.

After a while, their relationship dissolved. I went back to work part time. One day, I got a call from the police that her husband climbed into my window to threaten her. I had to leave work to tend to the situation. He wanted her back and she was not opposed to being back with him. The police asked me if I wanted to press charges. I said no on the strength of our friendship. Now he was living with us and working at Mc Donald's. I always gave him a ride to work and picked him up. The whole time they stayed with me they never offered me a dime. Her husband liked to drink and smoke crack. There would be days, like pay days, she wouldn't hear from him. That was none of my business. Marie made friends with a neighbor of mine. She would go to her house and hang out all day and sometimes sleep there.

To be honest, it felt like she was planning her next move to get in good and then move in with her, but she never did. The lady would come to my house, visit, have coffee or we would go out at night when my mom would watch Amir. She didn't watch him often because she always said he acted up.

One night we went out. It was just me and Marie's friend. We were walking from the bar, and I complimented a guy. Next thing I knew, I had four girls wanting to fight me. We got into a brief tussle. Then, they called the cops on me. Marie's friend did nothing to help me. I had four girls and a guy I was fighting off. I held my own.

The cops came to question me. I told them what happened and that they attacked me. One of the girls was yelling across the cop car. I never liked the word "nigga." It was a trigger. I ran from the cop, got a hold of her, and beat her badly. I blacked out. Next thing I knew, I was fighting the cops. It took seven of them to get me in cuffs. I was charged with assault on the woman and a few counts of assault on the police. I was booked. They took all my gold chains, bracelets, and money from my jacket. I was given a phone call. I called home and told them my bail was $200.00. I told them the money was in my tall black boots.

I had to spend the night, but in the morning, they could come to the police station to bail me out. It was Sunday morning; Marie and her friend came and bailed me out. They gave me my personal things. All my money was gone from my jacket. It was a couple of hundred dollars! All my jewelry was missing. I went back and filed a complaint, but they told me it was never with my personal belongings. I was so pissed. I had thousands of dollars' worth of gold jewelry that disappeared. I never recouped anything. My complaint went nowhere.

I asked Marie's friend why she didn't do anything to help me when they jumped me. All she could say was, "You were handling your own." That's why I never called her my friend; she was shady.

Marie ended up moving in with her because I spoke my mind and said it was time for her and her husband to go. We were still cool. I would go to visit her a couple of doors down, but there was some tension with her friend.

Summer arrived. It was hot. Marie came over and told me she was moving to Virginia to live with her niece. I was shocked and felt like I was losing my best friend. I thought about it and offered to drive down. I kept my house. I planned to stay with my kids' aunt who was in the navy. We packed up the car the next day and headed out. We stayed at her niece's house the first few days. Then, she drove me to my kids' aunt's house. I had to quickly learn how to navigate to other parts of the city. Marie stayed 30 minutes from me. I would go hang out there with Amir during the day.

Then, after a month, Marie asked if her niece could pay me money to stay at my house. I said, "Sure, why not?" She moved in and would send the money through Western Union to stay there every month. I found a job with an in-house room to live in free of charge.

I was doing similar work that I was doing in Rhode Island. The house was a mess. I spent several days deep cleaning before I moved me and my son in. I also had to register him for school. I stayed busy and had no time to hang out with Marie. It was deplorable the way these adults with disabilities were living.

There was freezer burnt food from the food pantry, dirty sheets on the beds, roaches in the house, meds missing and not given. It was a husband and wife who owned several homes. They were surprised at my knowledge and how quickly I got that house up to living standards. They had to invest money but that's why they got money.

I only worked there for two to three months because my mom called me and told me they were repossessing my car because I missed payments. I also found out that I had high gas and electric bills. They were going to cut it off. I couldn't contact Marie's niece, but I had called Marie to tell her I was going back home. I was taking a train because I was scared to drive all that way by myself. I told her to drive me to the train station the next day and to keep the car there but take off my plates. I had given the bank the address.

Me and Amir took the train home. It was a 12-hour ride. We rode at night so we could sleep. Morning came and we were almost home. My mom was picking us up. We got off the train with our luggage and walked to the parking lot. I saw my mom and Jahmere. I gave him a hug and kiss and got into the front seat after buckling in Amir. I heard it all within the 25-minute car ride back to Newport.

Girl from the Wrong Side of the Tracks

My mom did not pull any punches when it came down to telling me I needed to get it together. We arrived home. No one was there. The house was clean. There was no trace of Marie's niece or her belongings. I made a phone call to the church that helped with bills. They told me to bring in both of my bills. Amir and I showered and went to the church. They didn't ask any questions. They just wrote a check for both bills and told me to call the company and tell them I would pay the balance due at the supermarket. I called my mom again for a ride to pay the bills at the local supermarket in Middletown, RI, five minutes from Newport. I paid the bills, got confirmation the bills were paid, and went to hang out at my mom's house to spend time with Jahmere. I asked him how summer school was going, and he said it was good. He was getting so tall and stocky, just like his dad. He looks so much like his dad. Amir looked more like me but had his dad's lips.

We had dinner. Mom cooked on the grill. The boys played in the pool, and we ate. Then, after dinner I went home. I unpacked our clothes and re-washed them because they smelled like the house in Virginia. When the laundry was done, I called it a night. I woke up the next morning and my aunt Lea came over. We chatted. She told me how I could claim bankruptcy for five hundred dollars. I didn't tell her I was going to do it, but when I got my next check, I went to see the lawyer and showed him all my bills. It was official, I filed Chapter 7 Bankruptcy.

I had a clean slate. It took me a few months to get on my feet. I bought a used car. I knew I had to get it together. I didn't do half of the shit I was doing. The only problem was, I had another "can you do me a favor?" It was my cousin. He was under house arrest and wanted to use my address to get out of prison. I said, "Sure."

Self-Medicating

Within a few days my cousin moved into the back room that was Jahmere's. It was fine, but with that came his friends, drinking and smoking weed. He had girls come over to have sex. He was the true essence of a man. I would drink from time to time. It was not out of control.

On July 4, 2003, I was on another drunken binge. I did not have either of my kids with me this day. I started the day off by buying a big bottle of Absolute Vodka and went to 7-Eleven for cranberry juice. I sipped and played music. It was kind of early in the day.

Time passed and before I knew it, I had polished off the whole bottle and still didn't feel drunk. I wanted to kick it up a notch. I went upstairs to my room which had laundry on the floor and in the baskets. It was not as clean as I typically kept it. I went into my closet, in my stash basket, and took a few pills from each bottle. It was nothing major to me. I was used to popping these pills to get higher and have more fun. I went into my purse and grabbed some money. I had about $800.00 in cash, so I took $200.00 with me to go to the bar.

I hit a few bars on Broadway mid-day and had some more drinks with "friends." My favorite bartender was working so she knew what I wanted. They were strong like I liked it with a splash of juice. I had a few drinks and low and behold one of my one-time drunk night flings walked in. He bought me a drink and we chatted. That chat led to us going back to his apartment. We had sex. It meant nothing because I was just feeding my sexual desire. When I was done, I bounced on him quick.

I walked home. My cousin was there and said he was throwing a BBQ. I said, "Okay. There were a few dudes in the backyard, and a few in the living room and kitchen. I went upstairs to shower and wash the sex off me. I got dressed, took a few more pills. I don't remember what they were. I was supposed to take them every day, but I never did because I wasn't serious about my treatment. I went downstairs and took a little nap. No doubt, the pills say do not drink with alcohol! For me, that was just a bigger high and I liked the way it made me feel.

I woke up still woozy. I had a feeling of being depressed because I was not with my kids, my friends or family. I called my mother. She said she had company and wasn't doing anything big. I don't recall what my response was in full detail, but I said, "Okay, I'm having a cook-out." She said, "Good for you," and we hung up. I tried to call a few more friends but didn't get an answer. I called my right-hand girl, and still no answer. I felt so alone and depressed. I went to the liquor store again for another big bottle of Absolute. I got back home and poured a drink with a splash of cranberry juice over a few ice cubes. There was more liquor than any other content in my tall glass. I went outside and hung out with everyone else.

We were laughing. My cousin said, "Yo, cousin, you look smashed." I said, "Nah, I'm good." All along, inside, I'm not feeling so well. I was feeling depressed; I had fleeting thoughts of killing myself. I had the weight of the world on my shoulders. I was missing Mark. My backyard faced his old house and I now lived next door to where Jayceon lived.

I always carried a knife with me after that fight I got in a month ago. I wasn't taking any chances. I was out of my mind. My cousin was ready to start the grill. He sent me in to get the charcoal fluid. For whatever reason, I got it, grabbed my drink, my cigarettes, and went up to my room. I locked the door behind me, sat on my bed, and just was going crazy. My mind was bugging out. I had thoughts of suicide. I heard voices. I sprayed the cloth on the floor with charcoal fluid. I went into the closet to grab my stash of pills. I took them all and finished my drink. The basket was empty on the bed. I dozed off for a minute, or God knows how long.

I got up, lost my balance, and there went the charcoal fluid. I lit a cigarette with a book of matches and threw it in the ash tray. I smoked my cigarette. All I could hear was, "You're going to die, bitch." The voice kept repeating itself. "You're going to burn, bitch." This happened a few times. It was like I was no longer in control of my actions. I dropped one match on the floor and passed out on the bed.

I woke up to the fire on the floor and the baskets. I was so afraid from that and the pounding on my door. I hid in the closet. The fire grew bigger, and the banging continued. Was this the way I was going to die? I pulled out my knife and sliced my wrist…

Made in the USA
Middletown, DE
23 July 2024

57867804R00064